FROM FIELD TO FOREST

The Discovering Nature Series
General Editor: Dr. Phyllis S. Busch

In the same series by
Phyllis S. Busch and Arline Strong

From Field to Forest

HOW PLANTS AND ANIMALS
CHANGE THE LAND

Text and photographs by
Laurence Pringle

THE WORLD PUBLISHING COMPANY
NEW YORK AND CLEVELAND

All the photographs in this book are by Laurence Pringle, with the exception of those on pages 10, 12, 44, and 47, which are reproduced by courtesy of Arline Strong. The publishers gratefully acknowledge permission to use these photographs.

Published by The World Publishing Company
110 East 59th Street, New York, New York 10022
Published simultaneously in Canada by
Nelson, Foster & Scott Ltd.
Library of Congress catalog card number: 79–101840
Text copyright © 1970 by Laurence Pringle
Illustrations copyright © 1970 by Laurence Pringle
Printed in the United States of America.
Designed by Jack Jaget

FOR HEIDI,
WHO WOULD RATHER BE SWIMMING

EDITOR'S FOREWORD

This book is planned to encourage the very young child to
experience his environment aesthetically as well as intellectually—
with his heart as well as his mind.
The approach is intended to stimulate children to learn by
inquiry rather than by mere passive acceptance of stated facts.
Thus the child is led to explore for himself the
wonders and beauty of the world of nature.
From Field to Forest is one of a series of books designed
to acquaint young children with the interrelationships which exist
among living things and their environment. These books
explain how plants and animals (including man) affect their
surroundings and how they, in turn, are themselves affected.
An understanding of these interrelationships is essential in order
that children may appreciate that people are only part of
nature and not masters of nature.
From Field to Forest is about the changes in plant and animal life
which take place on land that was once cultivated, then abandoned.

PHYLLIS S. BUSCH

Perhaps you play in an open field near your home.
Imagine coming back to visit the field many years from now.
What would the land be like?

You might find
a forest growing there.

Everything changes in nature,
and fields often change into forests.
Watching this change is like
watching a very slow parade.
The "marchers" are different
kinds of plants.
One kind of plant grows for a time,
then is replaced, or *succeeded,*
by another.
The parade is called *plant succession.*

This book shows some kinds
of changes you might see on fields
in parts of the eastern United States.
The changes will be different
in other parts of the country.

If you visit a field
where the soil is bare,
you can watch to see the parade
of plants begin.

As long as the soil receives
sunlight and rain, plants can grow.
In a bare field, some plants
may sprout from seeds and roots
that are already in the soil.
Other plants—such as dandelions—
sprout from seeds newly carried
to the field by the wind.

The first plants in a field are those that grow well in the open sunlight. Ragweed, dandelion, and crabgrass quickly cover the bare soil.

Most of these "pioneer" plants die when winter comes.
But they leave seeds that will sprout the following spring.
Sometimes you can find seeds on the dead plant stalks that stick above the snow.

Each year new kinds of plants begin to grow in the field.
Among the first are thistle and milkweed.
Their seeds have light, fluffy "hairs" and are easily carried to the field by the wind.

In just a few years, you might find bushes, shrubs, and small trees like chokecherry growing in a field that has been left to change.

The seeds of these plants are too heavy
to be carried by the wind.
Often they are brought to the field by birds.
A bird may accidentally drop a berry
from its beak as it flies over.
Often when a bird eats some fruit, the seeds
pass through its body and become part
of the bird's wastes, or droppings.
Bushes or shrubs may sprout
where the droppings fall.

Most of the new plants in the field could not begin to grow on hot, bare soil.
But the pioneer plants have shaded the soil.
In this shade, the seeds of tall grasses, weeds, and shrubs
have a chance to sprout and grow.

Once started, the new kinds of plants grow thick and tall.
Beneath them, the pioneer plants get little light from the sun.
Their seeds may not sprout in the cool shade. They begin to die out.
After a few years all of the pioneer plants are gone.
They are replaced by plants that live for two years or more.

Look for a field like this.

It is an exciting place to explore.

You may find colorful flowers such as brown-eyed Susans, daisies, teasel, and Queen Anne's lace.

You may find bushes with delicious raspberries.

And you are sure to find many animals.

In a bare field there are few hiding places and little food for animals.
But as soon as the soil is covered with pioneer plants,
the field begins to attract animals.
A woodchuck may dig its den in the field and feed on grasses and other plants.
You might see the woodchuck looking out of its burrow.

At night,
a family of skunks may visit the field,
catching earthworms and crickets,
or digging in the soil for grubs.

As the numbers and kinds of plants in the field increase,
so do the animals.
All sorts of insects live in the field.
Many are plant-eaters, such as grasshoppers and katydids.

The plant-eating insects are hunted by praying mantises and field spiders.
You can hunt for them too.

Butterflies and bees
fly from flower to flower,
sipping sweet nectar
or gathering pollen.

Meadowlarks and song sparrows
nest in the field and find
insect food there.
You might find the nest of a
red-winged blackbird if the field
is near a pond or marsh.

The field is full of life.
Take a step, and a meadow mouse
scurries away
along its grass-covered trackway.
Take a few more steps
and you may see a
cottontail rabbit watching you.

Look closely at the plants around you.
Do you see something that looks like spit on a plant stem?
Poke at the wet bubbles with your finger.
Hidden in the spit you will find a tiny green insect—a young spittlebug.
Set the spittlebug on a grass stem.
Then watch to see how it builds a new house of froth around itself.

For a long time, tiny seeds from pine trees have been dropped in the field by the wind.
If you look among the thick grasses and weeds, you will find young trees beginning to grow.
Pine trees can grow very quickly.
Once they reach higher than the surrounding weeds, they thrive in the sunlight.
As they grow taller and their branches spread wide,
the pines cast shade on the plants below.
Cut off from the sun, plants like goldenrod and berry bushes begin to die out.
After a few years, a young pine forest may cover the field.
The colorful weeds are gone.
So are most of the animals that lived among them.
Many field animals cannot survive in a pine forest.

Other kinds of animals
live among the pines.
Deer hide there.
Cardinals and doves
build their nests on pine branches.

White-footed mice
find seeds and insects
on the forest floor.

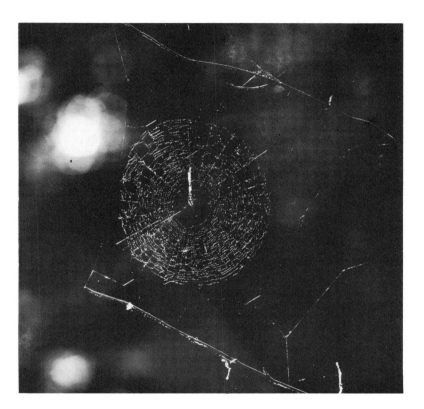

And forest spiders
spin their webs
and catch insects that fly
among the pine trees.

Beneath the pines
the ground is carpeted with leaves,
called needles, that drop from the tree
Very little sunlight
reaches the floor of the young forest.
The lower branches of the pines die
for lack of light.
Only a few kinds of plants
such as ferns and mushrooms
can live in the dim light.

As the years pass, the pine trees grow to be a hundred feet tall or more.
They produce seeds, and the seeds sail down to the cool forest floor.
But very few pine seeds become trees.
They sprout and grow for a time but then die.
They need plentiful sunlight in order to stay alive.
They also need water, and get little because the roots of the big pines
take up most of the water near the top of the soil.

But oaks and hickories can grow
in the shade of a pine forest.
Their seeds reach the pine woods
by accident, perhaps dropped by
a blue jay or buried by a squirrel.
Many of the young trees die
before they have grown more than
a few inches, but others keep alive.
Their roots grow below the roots
of the big pine trees, and bring
water from deep in the soil.

When a pine tree dies,
sunlight can reach the young
oak and hickory trees
near the forest floor.
Their growth speeds up.
As more and more of the old pines die,
their places are taken by the trees
that have been waiting below.
The parade of plants goes on.
After many years, an oak-hickory forest grows
where the pines, and the weeds,
and the pioneer plants,
and the bare soil used to be.

With the change in plant life there is a change in animal life.
Now you will see gray squirrels or fox squirrels
feeding on acorns and hickory nuts.
They could not live in a pine forest.

The little pine woods tree frog
that clung to the trunks of the evergreens is gone.
Toads hop upon the dead oak leaves that now cover the forest floor.

Roaming the forest floor, box turtles hunt for berries and insects.
And at night, the pale green luna moth flies through the woods like a small ghost.

It may take a hundred and fifty years
for a bare field
to change to an oak-hickory forest.
After that, the forest will continue
to look much the same,
though some changes will take place.
Acorns will fall to the ground,
sprout, and begin to grow.
When a great oak
crashes to the ground,
small oaks will be ready to replace it.

An oak-hickory forest
can go on like this for centuries.
Then it may be destroyed by a
forest fire, a windstorm, or by man.
If the land is then left alone,
the parade of plants
will start once more.
Many years later, the land will again
be covered by an oak-hickory forest.

Not all fields change into forests of oaks and hickories.
The parade of plants differs from place to place.
In some areas, the forests are mostly spruce and fir trees.

In some parts
of the northern United States
there are no pines or
other evergreens in the parade.
Here, a young maple you find in the grass
may someday be part of a maple-beech forest.

Along parts of the Pacific coast
a field may change to a redwood forest.

And in some parts of the central United States
there is so little rain that few trees can grow.
Instead, a field of bare soil
changes to a prairie.

What will your favorite field look like
many years from now?
To find out, visit young forests
and old forests in the same neighborhood.
Watch the changes happening there.
The parade of plants and animals you see
is marching across the land all around you.

ABOUT THE AUTHOR

LAURENCE PRINGLE is executive editor of The American Museum of Natural
History's magazine for young readers, *Nature and Science.* He is the author
and photographer of many articles on wildlife, and has written
two other books for young readers. He has also been a teacher,
and has a B.S. and an M.S. degree in wildlife conservation.
Mr. Pringle is married and lives in northern New Jersey.